Color & Cook
CUPCAKES

MONICA WELLINGTON

D1621510

DOVER PUBLICATIONS, INC.
MINEOLA, NEW YORK

For Lydia and Shelby,
the great cupcake bakers

Note

Coloring is fun, and so is cooking—and in this delightful book, you'll get to do both! First, meet Molly and Jack, who are baking delicious cupcakes. You'll see them choose a recipe, get their ingredients and cooking tools together, and then bake their cupcakes in the oven—with the help of their mother, because it's important to be safe in the kitchen. You will also find cupcake ideas for every month of the year, as well as recipes for cupcakes and frosting. Are you ready for a delicious adventure? Let's get started!

Bibliographical Note

Color & Cook CUPCAKES is a new work, first published by Dover Publications, Inc., in 2009.

DOVER *Pictorial Archive* SERIES

This book belongs to the Dover Pictorial Archive Series. You may use the designs and illustrations for graphics and crafts applications, free and without special permission, provided that you include no more than four in the same publication or project. (For permission for additional use, please write to Permissions Department, Dover Publications, Inc., 31 East 2nd Street, Mineola, N.Y. 11501.)

However, republication or reproduction of any illustration by any other graphic service, whether it be in a book or in any other design resource, is strictly prohibited.

International Standard Book Number
ISBN-13: 978-0-486-47113-6
ISBN-10: 0-486-47113-6

Manufactured in the United States of America
Dover Publications, Inc., 31 East 2nd Street, Mineola, N.Y. 11501

Molly and Jack love to bake!
Today they're picking a favorite cupcake recipe from their cookbook.

Molly and Jack get ready to make the cupcakes.
They get out their equipment and utensils.

wooden spoon

rubber spatula

electric beater

mixing bowls

fork knife spoon

apron

sifter

baker's hat

measuring cup

measuring spoons

paper baking cups

potholder

potholder mitt

plastic measuring cups

timer

cupcake pan

Can you help them find all of these things in their kitchen?

They take out the ingredients that they need for the cupcake recipe.

Can you help them find all of these ingredients in their kitchen?

Jack and Molly carefully follow the steps in the recipe. They count and measure.

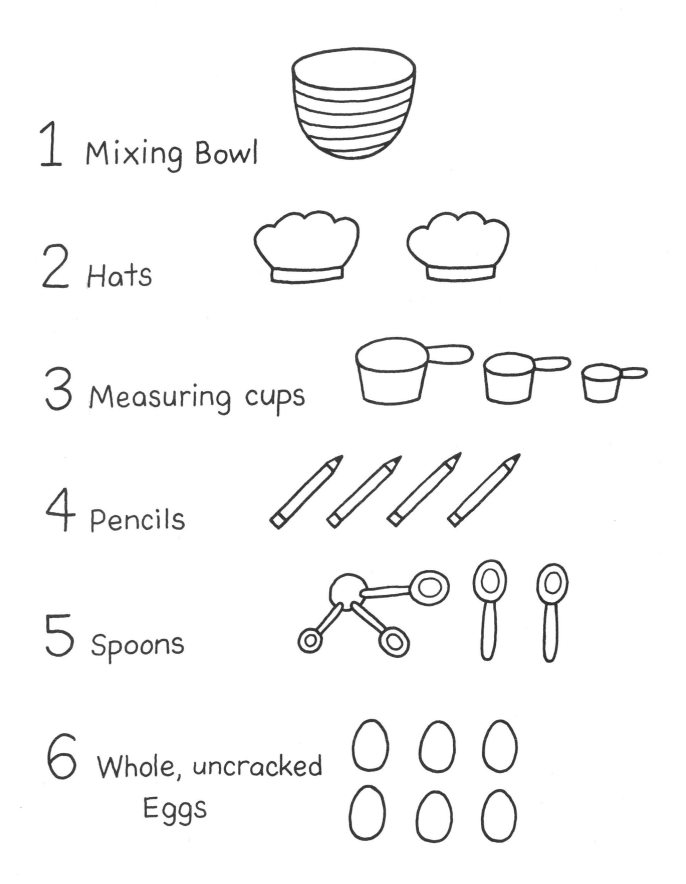

1 Mixing Bowl

2 Hats

3 Measuring cups

4 Pencils

5 Spoons

6 Whole, uncracked Eggs

Can you find all of these items in their kitchen? Make sure you find the right number of each.

Jack and Molly use the electric beater to mix the batter until it's smooth.
Mom keeps an eye on what they are doing in the kitchen.

Molly puts the paper baking cups into the cupcake pan.
Jack puts a big spoonful of batter into each cup.

Mom helps them put the cupcakes into the oven to bake.
She is careful because the oven is very hot. They set the timer.

There is a lot to clean up in the kitchen.
They do the dishes and put everything back in the cupboards and drawers.

11

Bring-Bring! The timer goes off. The cupcakes are perfectly baked.
Out they come from the oven, nicely browned.

Wow! They smell good!

While the cupcakes cool, Jack and Molly get ready to decorate them.
They make the frosting. They have lots of decorations to set out.

14

Sprinkles

Marshmallows

Candy corn

Peppermint sticks

Strawberries

Cherries

Candy hearts

Nuts

Apple slices

Blueberries

Licorice

Jelly beans

Gumdrops

Chocolate chips

Coconut

Paper umbrellas

Paper flags

Candles

Can you help them find all of these decorations in their kitchen?

Jack starts by putting frosting on a cupcake.

Molly decorates a cupcake with colored sprinkles.
There are many different colors to choose from.

Jack and Molly have lots of ideas for decorating their cupcakes.
Can you help them?

ladybug

panda

pig

lion

frog

bee

mouse

bunny

cat

They turn the cupcakes into funny animals, using colored frosting and different decorations. Can you make some, too?

January

Make a snowman with marshmallows. Use shredded coconut for snow.

February

Make Valentine's Day cupcakes with lots of heart-shaped candies and red sprinkles.

March

Make a St. Patrick's Day cupcake with green gumdrops for shamrocks.

April

Play tricks on April Fool's Day! Put an apricot half on white frosting. It looks like a real egg!

May

Birds are building nests in the spring. Put jelly beans or chocolate eggs in your bird's nest.

June

It is fun to make flower cupcakes with gumdrops and brightly colored candies.

It is fun to celebrate holidays and special occasions.
Jack and Molly make cupcakes for each month of the year.

July

Red, white and blue for July 4th! Decorate with blueberries, raspberries, and strawberries on white frosting.

August

Make cool summer cupcakes with fish gummies swimming on blue frosting.

September

Apple-picking time! Put apple slices on your cupcake. (A squeeze of lemon juice will keep the slices fresh.)

October

Halloween time: witches, black cats, and spiders can have licorice legs.

November

Candy corn and pumpkins are yummy for Thanksgiving cupcakes.

December

Make snowflake cupcakes with stencils.

You can make up your own holiday cupcakes, too!

Molly and Jack have made lots of great cupcakes.
What do you think they're getting ready for?

Look! Friends are coming to their house.

It's a PARTY! There are lots of cupcakes for everyone!

Which ones would you choose? Yummy! Cupcakes are delicious!

Recipes

Applesauce Cupcakes

(Makes 12 cupcakes)

$\frac{1}{2}$ cup softened butter ($\frac{1}{2}$ cup vegetable oil can be substituted)

1 cup sugar

2 eggs

1 $\frac{1}{4}$ cups flour

$\frac{1}{2}$ teaspoon baking soda

$\frac{1}{2}$ teaspoon salt

1 teaspoon cinnamon

$\frac{1}{2}$ teaspoon nutmeg

1 cup applesauce

1. Preheat oven to 350 degrees.
2. Cream together butter (or oil) and sugar in a large mixing bowl.
3. Add eggs and beat well.
4. In a separate bowl, mix together the flour, baking soda, spices, and salt.
5. Add dry mixture to creamed mixture alternately with the applesauce, beating after each addition and blending well.
6. Place paper baking cups into muffin tray and pour in batter until each cup is about $\frac{3}{4}$ full.
7. Bake for 30 minutes, or until a toothpick inserted into a cupcake comes out clean.
8. Cool before icing with Vanilla Frosting.

Vanilla Frosting

2 tablespoons softened butter

2 cups confectioners sugar

1 teaspoon vanilla extract

3 tablespoons milk

1. Cream together butter, sugar, and vanilla extract.
2. Add milk and stir well, until smooth and easy to spread.

Note: Children should always have the assistance of an adult for help and safety.

Recipes

Carrot Cupcakes

(Makes 12 cupcakes)

> ½ cup softened butter (½ cup vegetable oil can be substituted)
> 1 cup sugar
> 2 eggs
> 1 cup grated carrots
> 1¼ cups flour
> ½ teaspoon baking soda
> 1 teaspoon cinnamon
> ½ teaspoon salt

1. Preheat oven to 350 degrees.
2. Cream together butter and sugar in a large mixing bowl.
3. Add eggs and beat well.
4. Mix in grated carrots.
5. In a separate bowl, mix together the flour, baking soda, cinnamon, and salt.
6. Add dry mixture to creamed mixture, beating after each addition and blending well.
7. Place paper baking cups into muffin tray and pour in batter until each cup is about ¾ full.
8. Bake for 30 minutes, or until a toothpick inserted into a cupcake comes out clean.
9. Cool before icing with Cream Cheese Frosting.

Cream Cheese Frosting

> ⅓ of 8-oz. package of cream cheese
> 1 tablespoon softened butter
> ½ teaspoon vanilla extract
> 1 cup confectioners sugar

1. With an electric mixer, beat cream cheese and butter until well blended.
2. Add vanilla extract and beat in.
3. Gradually add sugar, and beat until smooth and slightly fluffy.

Note: Children should always have the assistance of an adult for help and safety.

Recipes

Chocolate Cupcakes

(Makes 12 cupcakes)

½ cup softened butter
½ cup white sugar
½ cup brown suga
1 teaspoon vanilla extract
2 eggs
1 cup flour

½ cup unsweetened cocoa powder
½ teaspoon baking soda
½ teaspoon baking powder
½ teaspoon salt
½ cup plain non-fat yogurt

1. Preheat oven to 350 degrees.
2. Cream together butter, white sugar, and brown sugar in a large mixing bowl.
3. Add eggs and vanilla extract and beat well.
4. In a separate bowl, mix together the flour, cocoa powder, baking soda, baking powder, and salt.
5. Add dry mixture to creamed mixture alternately with the yogurt, beating after each addition and blending well.
6. Place paper baking cups into muffin tray and pour in batter until each cup is about ¾ full.
7. Bake for 25 minutes, or until a toothpick inserted into a cupcake comes out clean.
8. Let cool before icing with Chocolate Frosting (or Vanilla Frosting or Cream Cheese Frosting).

Chocolate Frosting

1½ cups confectioners sugar
⅓ cup unsweetened cocoa powder
2 tablespoons melted butter
½ teaspoon vanilla extract
3 tablespoons milk

1. Combine confectioners sugar and cocoa powder.
2. Create a small well in the middle of the dry mixture and add melted butter, vanilla extract, and milk.
3. Blend well, until smooth and easy to spread.

Note: Children should always have the assistance of an adult for help and safety.

Recipes

Vanilla Cupcakes

(Makes 12 cupcakes)

   ½ cup softened butter
   1 cup sugar
   2 eggs
   ½ cup milk
   1 teaspoon vanilla extract
   1½ cups flour
   1 teaspoon baking powder
   ½ teaspoon salt

1. Preheat oven to 350 degrees
2. Cream together butter and sugar in a large mixing bowl.
3. Add eggs, milk and vanilla extract and beat well.
4. In a separate bowl, mix together the flour, baking powder, and salt.
5. Add dry mixture to creamed mixture, beating after each addition and blending well.
6. Place paper baking cups into muffin tray and pour in batter until each cup is about ¾ full.
7. Bake for 30 minutes, or until a toothpick inserted into a cupcake comes out clean.
8. Let cupcakes cool before icing with Lemon Frosting (or Chocolate Frosting, Vanilla Frosting or Cream Cheese Frosting).

Lemon Frosting

   1 cup confectioners sugar
   Juice and zest of ½ small lemon
   2 tablespoons softened butter

1. Grate lemon zest and squeeze lemon juice into the sugar.
2. Mix and let sit for about 15 minutes.
3. Beat in butter, until smooth and easy to spread. (If too thin, add a little more sugar to make a good spreading consistency)

If you choose, you can make your cupcakes colorful with sprinkles!

Note: Children should always have the assistance of an adult for help and safety.

That was fun!

ML   6/09